HEELS WITH POWER

Walking in Victory in the Face of Adversity

HEELS WITH POWER

Walking in Victory in the Face of Adversity

by

Diane Parker

Williams and King Publishers

ISBN: 978-0-9983663-9-5
       0998366390

Printed in the USA

All scripture is quote in the King James Version unless otherwise noted.

The spelling of the proper noun satan with a lower case "s" is intentional

Dedication

To women everywhere secretly battling the emotional stress of lost dreams, identity, self-respect and worth - I dedicate this book to you. In the midst of your feelings of rejection, betrayal, guilt and shame, may you find the strength and courage to take off your mask, surrender your will and rest safe in the arms of God. You too can stand with dignity, grace and power during any storm.

Acknowledgments

I would not have been able to bare the difficult times without the prayers and support of the wonderful people God has placed in my life. I am grateful to Him for my family and friends whose love, prayers and support kept me fighting when I wanted to quit. Even when you did not understand my journey, you did not disown me. You loved me in the midst of it. I will forever be grateful to you all.

To my husband, even during your struggles, you have always encouraged me to pursue my dreams and to be all that God has called me to be. You've prayed with me, laughed with me and cried with me. You believed in me even when you did not believe in yourself. I pray God's richest blessings upon you and that you find the peace, rest and wholeness I have found in Him.

To God, my Father. I love you so much. Thank you for your unconditional love. You are my refuge, you are my strength, you are my strong tower. You are my immovable rock. In you I have found a safe haven. You have given me life. All thanks, praise, honor and glory to you for making this possible!

Table of Contents

Bishop Clint S. Brown

Foreward

Everyone experiences failure in life. Many have walked the path lost. Very few have the POWER to get back up on their feet, face the storm and decide not to quit or give up.

Diane Parker is one of the resilient warriors that did just that. In this incredible book she takes us all on her journey of Trials and Triumphs that not only gave her the strength to keep going, but also gives us strategies so we can do the same.

I've heard it said, "There are three kinds of people in the world. Those who have been through a storm, those who are in a storm and those who are headed for one.

In this awesome book Diane reminds us that we don't have to live another day as a prisoner without freedom when deep down we know we were born to Rule and Reign.

So get ready to let go of your past and walk into your future with your head held high, and don't forget to put on your HEELS WITH POWER!

Introduction

"You look good, you feel good" - that was the motto I lived by. No matter how I felt. If I could put on a pair of heels, a nice suit or dress and look like I had it all together, that is all I needed to do. In fact, people would come to know me by "my heels." Upon greeting me they always looked at my feet to see what pair I was wearing. I had a good paying job and money in the bank. I was married to my best friend. Life was good. We encountered problems here and there, but no more than most couples. God healed me from a chronic disease a few years prior so I was confident in my faith and trust in God. I was not prepared for what was coming next. Not only did a storm hit my life, it blew the door off the hinges and turned my life and marriage upside down.

Although I had some knowledge of my husband's past, I was not aware of the depth of his childhood pain and fears which led to his deep dark secret of sexual and drug addiction. I was devastated. The hopelessness and despair I felt was indescribable. I was angry and confused. I was overcome with embarrassment and shame. I discovered, no amount of material success or accomplishment could heal my bleeding soul. Buying a new pair of shoes was not going to fix this. Desperate to find relief from the overwhelming pain I felt within, I sought after God with my whole heart. I did not want a massage to make me feel better. I wanted to be free from the depths of my soul. Through my pain, I developed a hunger to know God and a thirst for His righteousness (1 Corinthians 10:13b "And God is faithful; He will not let you be tempted beyond what you can bear.") What I felt seemed unbearable, so I knew the only way to learn of His ways and divine purpose in my life was to spend time with Him. This is where my journey begins.

"Heels with Power" is a book of inspiration, strength, power and grace. In it I share my process and journey of hope and

healing in the midst of my loved one's addiction. Although I share events and the effects of his addiction, the same biblical principles can be applied in any circumstance or adversity you may face.

As women, we are told to look pretty, be strong, while living under the pressure of appearing as if we have it all together and silently battling emotional issues and feelings of betrayal, pain, shame, fear, etc. We are afraid that if we face our pain, it will overtake us and swallow us up. Instead we run and hide and remain silent. We put on our mask and live each day the best we can. I could no longer live this way. The pain was too great. When someone else has caused the crisis in your life, it is easy to blame our offender and remain stuck in the place of wanting our offender to suffer and pay for what was done to us. It was not until I took my eyes off my husband and took a long hard look at myself, facing my own weaknesses and shortcoming, I was able to relinquish everything to God allowing Him to move on my behalf. The things I learned about myself are immeasurable. The unconditional, everlasting love I found in God is matchless. I discovered there was only one way out and that was true intimacy with God. From that point on, the storm **within** me ceased which caused the storms **around** me to be of no avail.

My heels today not only represent outward beauty but also the inward strength, power and grace I walk in today. No longer a victim of my circumstance but a victor through Christ. It's a process and a journey that quite literally saved my life!

Chapter 1

The Face of Addiction

*M*ost people run or turn a deaf ear when they hear the word addiction. They don't want to deal with it and or are embarrassed about it; yet, it is destroying our families, marriages, business relationships, ministries and the lives of our loved ones. It is important that we identify what addiction is and its root cause.

Addiction Defined

An addiction is anything that consumes the focus of your attention, distracting you from God. An addiction will prevent you from facing yourself and from being emotionally available in relationships. Addictions are not limited to alcohol, drugs, and sex but can be anything from potato chips to work, from gambling to exercise. There are two general categories of addictions. They are chemical addictions; drugs, alcohol and cigarettes, and process addictions which include eating disorders, sexual addiction, work, codependency, people and relationships, love, self-harm. There is also feeling addictions; also defined as emotional addictions. Emotional/feeling addictions are the result of negative events we have faced in our lives which put us in a place of rage, fear and sadness. As a result, these emotions become our reaction to everything in life. Finally, thought addictions; lustful thoughts, unsettled mind, (never at rest), worry, non-stop talking and detailing.

Many people are in bondage to some form of addiction but because they function every day (without incidence); and are not bums on the street or blacked out behind the wheel of a car, they are deceived into believing they do not have a problem. You could very well be the nice lady who hands out the Kleenex tissue at church but is silently and shamefully battling an addiction.

Addiction knows no boundaries, be it status, lifestyle, or even faith. This is where the deception comes in. Think about some of those things you feel you can't live without. It can be the six pack or that joint you just have to have every day. Perhaps it's the credit card that maintains an outstanding balance each month due to your spending habit or, the long hours you spend at work each day neglecting your family and then arriving home at nine p. m. with a pile of work under your arm to complete. Then again, it could be the three and four phone calls you absolutely have to make to your significant other daily unrelated to work or emergencies, or the secret activities you engage in that would shock the friends you respect? The irrepressible need for online sex or porn magazines, those activities that could lead to your arrest if discovered - these are addictions.

---

*Our emotions crave for love, affirmation,
identity, significance and sense of value.*

Just as we reach for an anesthetic when we feel physical pain, the addictive cycle drives you to reach for something to help you when you feel emotional pain. Addictive agents such as alcohol, drugs, food, work, sex, pornography, shopping are used to stop the pain. As the addictive agent is used, it affects the "reward circuit" of the brain with the chemical messenger dopamine. The over stimulation of the reward circuit of the brain, causes the pleasurable "high" that causes the use of the drug repeatedly. It also changes the brain in the area of self-control and interferes with the ability to resist the intensity of the urge to continue the behavior.

Hosea 4:6 states, "My people are destroyed for lack of knowledge." Our lack of knowledge in the area of addictions has caused many to fail and to live defeated lives. II Corinthians 2:11 says, "Lest satan should get an advantage of us for we are not ignorant of his devices." If we do not understand the way the enemy operates through addictions and do not have any knowledge of what they are, he will forever have the ability to deceive us and cause us to miss out on the purpose God had intended for us and ultimately waste our lives.

May we not be so self-consumed and judgmental that we ignore our brothers and sisters in bondage that need our prayers. May we as believers walk in the power of the Holy Spirit in the authority we have in the name of Jesus and break the power of darkness off the lives of our loved ones, that they may find healing and wholeness in Christ.

Heels with Power

Chapter 2

Front Page

*E*arly on in our marriage all seemed fine. Who better to marry than your best friend? We shared common interests and spent hours at a time sharing about our day and other topics of concern and interest. I received a promotion on my job and began spending ten to twelve hours a day at work while leaving my husband alone. This was not a good thing! At the time, I did not realize all of the problems that would come as a result of it. I remember one evening in particular, my husband called me at work and asked when would I be home. He threatened to leave and go out if I did not come home within the hour. I explained to my boss that I had to go and so I left immediately. But… it was already too late. The cycle had already started in his mind. As I waited to be picked up from work the next day, my ride never came. I was left stranded. My husband decided that he was tired of being home alone and decided to act on his thoughts. He connected with some old friends and began drinking, using drugs and watching porn. I was very naïve to the drug world and its cycle. I did not understand how one minute everything could be okay and then in the next everything would be falling apart. I knew nothing about tough love or about enabling your spouse. All I knew was my husband had been complaining all the time about my long hours at work. He had spent our bill money and now he had left me stranded at work. Instead of recognizing the signs, I blamed myself for not being an attentive wife and spending too much time at work.

Pride and shame kept me silent. No one knew what I was facing. In fact, it happened several more times within a three-month period. He would leave work early and come home late. Finally, one day he took the car and was gone for three days. He called me on the third day and told me he was on the side of the road and he could not get home. I finally worked up the nerve to call my sister and told her the whole story. She came over to take me to get him and the car. As we proceeded walking in the parking lot, she saw the car parked in the corner. He was in the car with his head pressed against the window. He was dirty, smelly and stoned out of his mind. He had blown a lot of money. I pulled him out of the car, ripped off his clothes, and threw them away. I was both devastated and angry at the same time. When my sister left, I went into my closet and began to cry out to God. What had I gotten myself into?

Later after things calmed down, my husband apologized profusely about his behavior. He appeared remorseful and decided he should just leave. I agreed. Two weeks later he was back. He decided he did not want to be separated and promised things would be different. He decided he would change jobs and we would work out something so he would not be tempted to spend his money. He got a really wonderful job and we made an arrangement with the accountant and the manager that I would pick up his checks. This worked out perfectly for us. I changed jobs as well and returned to working normal hours. We also became more actively involved in our church which left little room for outside interference. The next three years were fairly calm even though I had emotionally shut down.

Healing Thought

The Lord is close to the brokenhearted; He rescues those whose spirits are crushed. (Psalms 34:18) NLT

Diane Parker

Chapter 3

My Life or His?

There's one thing I discovered in this process and it's this – if you have unresolved issues they will certainly come back to haunt you in some shape or form. The truth is, I had issues of abandonment and fear. The fear of being left stranded was ever present in my mind. My husband had many childhood issues of rejection and pain along with losses that had not been grieved. Sadly, over the years he had learned to numb his pain and anxieties through pornography and drugs. He had created his own fantasy world to relieve the stresses of life.

While assisting my brother with the preparations for his

11

wedding, I began to notice a change in my husband's behavior. He appeared to be very stressed but when I questioned him about it, he denied it and said he was ok. This lasted for about a week. Once the wedding was over I guess he felt he needed a break because two days after the wedding, he had disappeared. The cycle had begun, again. I came home to find several items missing from our home. I was devastated. I immediately packed up what was left and went to my sister's. I was afraid and did not know what to do. He called a few days later after he discovered where I was and asked me to come home. I refused and demanded that he get some help. He turned to his boss who recommended an upscale rehabilitation center.

During his consultation with the doctors at the center, they determined that his addiction did not require in-patient care and could be handled as day care. This way, he could attend twelve weeks of rehabilitation in the evenings and still maintain his day job. When I had my session with his doctor, he suggested that I move back home. He said, for the sake of his recovery, it was important that he had my full support. I was undoubtedly very upset and angry.

I wanted nothing to do with him. I wanted them to lock him up and throw away the key. I remember crying all the way to work asking God where was He, because He had promised me He would not ever leave me. Suddenly I heard a still small voice say, "I am still here, you have to trust me." Peace immediately filled my heart and soul.

The next nine months were very intense. My husband appeared to be committed to his recovery so we signed another year lease on our apartment. I wanted to believe that everything was going to be fine but I did not have peace within my heart. I became consumed with his recovery. I went to every meeting and attended every session. I wanted to know everything about the drug including the behavior patterns and triggers. Although it was good to gain knowledge of the addiction, I became even more consumed with it. I was determined that I was going to stop this cycle and I would not be affected by it ever again.

> *What I learned was, it doesn't matter what I want, if the one addicted is not committed to staying clean, he or she will not remain clean. It is their recovery.*

The mistake we made was to believe that by removing ourselves from what we felt was the "bad environment", that would solve the issue; only to discover that if you don't deal with what is going on within, it doesn't matter where you are, you **will** go back. Yes, you guessed it. He went back after nine months of clean time. We had just bought another car and signed a new lease. I was very upset. We had debt up to our ears. In fact, I didn't take responsibility for anything, instead I blamed him for everything. It was his fault that we were in debt. It was his fault that I was miserable.

I walked in the door of our home overwhelmed with grief. As I began to pray, I heard these words, "What are you going to do now, run again?" At that moment, I fell on my face before God and repented. I cried, "Oh God, this is not about him. This is about me."

The next few moments would change my life forever and began my journey of healing and restoration. I realized that I had been so consumed with my husband's addiction and life, I no longer had a life. My life had become enmeshed in his. I had neglected myself and the things I knew God had impressed upon me to do. I had wasted a year of my life running behind him, making sure he did not use, and trying to protect myself from the fear I felt within.

I could no longer be consumed by my husband's behavior. I realized that I was on the brink of an emotional breakdown and the Lord had stepped in to rescue me. I had to get a grip on what was happening to me and begin to focus on taking care of myself. The next few weeks I began to make preparations to make the necessary changes in my life. My husband had become irresponsible and consumed with fulfilling his own fleshly desires. It was not long before we separated and he left. I could no longer afford our apartment with my salary alone so I had to move out. I was devastated about having to move because we lived in an upscale complex and I did not want to give up the lifestyle and comfort of home to which I had grown accustomed. I was embarrassed and ashamed that I could not afford to pay the rent, then having to go to my landlord and explain my situation. I was even more embarrassed that I couldn't even pay all my bills.

In the middle of my turmoil, God was there directing my every step. He opened the door for me to get another apartment in the same area, a little smaller and more affordable. I did not have to pay a deposit and I was able to move in right away. I made arrangements with the management of my present complex to make payments for the next year to pay out my lease since I had to break it. My world was falling apart and I did not understand why, but I knew God's hand was in it somewhere. I swallowed my pride, dried my eyes and submitted to the journey set before me.

Healing Thought

God is a safe-house for the battered, a sanctuary during bad times. The moment you arrive you relax; you are never sorry you knocked. (Psalms 9:9-10 – Message Bible)

Chapter 4

Removing the Mask

Acknowledging and Admitting My Pain

I felt so alone. The church I attended did not have any kind of support system, so it was difficult for me to open up to anyone. I was very involved in my church as a front-line singer in the choir and a Certified Food Manager for the banquet functions of the church as well as various other tasks. I appeared fine outwardly, but deep inside I was dying. Growing up I was taught that you don't share your pain or fears. You are to remain strong at all times. Admitting pain or fears was a sign of weakness. So, whenever I felt pain or disappointment I would either go shopping or just go into a shell and shut down. Later in life I learned to throw myself in my work or in ministry. I became consumed with helping others with their problems and working long hours at my job. I did not realize that this was simply another way I used to numb myself from the pain I felt within.

As I settled into my 625 square foot apartment, I began to sit in my closet every morning and evening and talk to God. My wounds were so deep that sometimes all I could do was lay on the floor and moan. I just wanted the pain to stop. I began to read the Psalms and I saw how David boldly talked to God about his pain and sought God's help. Psalms 25:15-17 jumped off the page as I read it. David said, "My eyes are ever toward the Lord, for He will pluck my feet out of the net. Lord turn to me and be gracious to me, for I am lonely and afflicted. The troubles of my heart have enlarged me. O bring me out of distress."

David laid before God the condition of his troubled mind. He expressed his dependence upon God and prayed earnestly for relief. He was honest about how he felt. He admitted that his problems were overtaking him and overwhelming him.

As I began to meditate on this scripture I began to weep uncontrollably. I realized that while I had learned in my walk with the Lord, to trust Him for my healing and my finances, when it came to my heart issues, I kept those to myself. I did not know how to trust God with heart issues. I became so good at hiding my emotions that I even hid them from myself. Eventually, by surrendering my wounded heart to God, I was able to release all the hurt and all the pain that was rooted deep within me. You see, you must reach a point in your life where you are sick and tired of being sick and tired. You must be tired of being depressed, tired of being angry and upset and tired of being hurt and frustrated. You have to, once and for all, become tired of the pain that has ruled your life. I had reached that point. And, unknown to me at the time, the sense of shame I had learned to live with was soon to be exposed.

The Face of Shame

Shame wears many faces. It demands to be hidden. It affects your thoughts and behavior. It causes you to live behind a smoke screen often acting as if nothing bothers you. It can rob you of your quality of life, hindering you from living life freely. It builds false or altered personalities with lies that say, "I am not hurting", when I really am or "I don't need any one", when I really do. Shame also taunts us by asking, "What's wrong with me? Why can't I be like so and so? Why do I continue to fail?"

It's easy to live with a sense of shame but deny the presence of it in our lives. Not only do you take on the shame of someone else's mistakes or behavior, but you become ashamed of yourself for being subjected to it. Ultimately you assume a shame-based identity. Shame becomes the core of your being. Everything in your life becomes poisoned by your emotions. You try desperately to do right so you can feel right, but the truth is, you fail each time. You become so ashamed of yourself it eventually leads to self-rejection. You constantly reject your real self, trying to be someone or something you are not.

You may also reject certain parts of yourself that are

displeasing to you. Shame is usually the root cause of many of our inner problems and compulsive behaviors such as drug and alcohol abuse, eating disorders, addiction to money and work, sexual perversion, the excessive need to be in control, lack of self-control or self-discipline, gossiping, a judgmental spirit, depression and a lack of confidence, just to name a few. New shame is then added on top of the shame you are already carrying. For years I lived with shame – hiding it even from myself. However, as I continued to surrender to Him, He began to reveal my deep-rooted feelings of unworthiness from being violated at an early age. It's amazing how shame can suddenly take over your entire being and overshadow everything. The embarrassment and shame I felt from my husband's behavior began to overwhelm me, compounded by my own shame because I was subjected to it. By this time, I was wondering what I had done wrong.

When I finally recognized and admitted to the fact that I had been living with a great deal of shame for so many years, it was through the power of the Holy Spirit I began to experience the immense and intense love God had for me. I was the apple of His eyes. And, as I continued to meditate on His love for me I understood then that I did not have to live with any shame.

Isaiah 61:7 (Amplified) says, "Instead of your (former) shame you shall have a twofold recompense; instead of dishonor and reproach (your people) shall rejoice in their portion. Therefore, in their land they shall possess double (what they had forfeited); everlasting joy shall be theirs." God says He will see to it that you are repaid for every injustice done to you. You will receive double for what you have lost and everlasting joy will be yours. Isaiah 54:4 (Amplified) says, "Fear not, for you shall not be ashamed; neither be confounded and depressed, for you shall not be put to shame. For you shall forget the shame of your youth, and you shall not (seriously) remember the reproach of your widowhood anymore."

Healing Thought

---

*No one who hopes in you will ever be put to
shame. (Psalms 25:3a – NIV)*

Heels with Power

26

Chapter 5

Come Clean with God

Time to Repent

*P*salms 25:18 (Amplified) states, "Behold my affliction and my pain and forgive all my sins (of thinking and doing). Often, we fail to see ourselves as responsible as the offender for certain actions. While it was not my fault that I was mistreated and emotionally abused, my reaction to it was my responsibility. When we have been wronged, we tend to feel justified in our anger or bitterness. I had to repent for my feelings of anger and resentment, bitterness and shame. I did not want my prayers to be hindered, nor did I want to miss out on what God had for me. Psalms 66:18 says, "If I regard iniquity in my heart, the Lord will not hear me."

Unconfessed sin is like carrying around a heavy garbage bag. I had to get my thinking aligned correctly with God.

Co- Dependent
Facing My Need to Be in Control

Having the responsibility at an early age for my sisters and brothers, I took on the role of mother and became consumed with taking care of everyone and everything. The unresolved issues from my childhood compounded by my husband's addiction caused me to try to take the place of God as savior and rescuer in his life. I assumed responsibility for his life instead of allowing him to be accountable and responsible for his own negative actions and behaviors.

I was what you would call a co-dependent even though I had never even heard the word before. I sadly discovered that it is not even used very often among believers and because of that, many women are unaware that they are in codependent relationships. I was one of them. It is quite natural to want to help the people we care about, but it is unhealthy to become consumed with fixing their lives. Beloved, God never intended for us to meet all the needs of others. Codependency will cause you to live in denial by pretending your circumstances are not as bad as they really are. You will put up with unacceptable behavior. When you're consumed with someone else's life, it enables you to avoid thinking about or facing your own feelings and issues. According to John Steadman Rice's book, *A Disease of One's Own – Psychotherapy, Addiction and Emergence of Co-Dependency*, some of the characteristics and behavioral patterns associated with co-dependency are:

- *assumes responsibility for others' feelings and behavior*
- *afraid of being hurt or rejected by others*
- *other people's actions and attitudes determine how you respond or react*
- *feel overly responsible for the feelings and behavior of others*
- *worry or fear how others may respond to your feelings*
- *put other people's needs and wants before your neglecting to take care of yourself*
- *fear of others' feelings of anger determine what you say or do*
- *judge what you do, think or say by someone else's standards*
- *anticipates other people's needs*

- *over commit yourself*
- *find yourself attracted to needy people*
- *seeking to be someone else's savior*
- *feel a sense of self-worth from helping others*
- *not allowing loved one to suffer consequences of negative behavior*
- *continue to give long after it hurts*
- *puts trusts in untrustworthy people*
- *looks for happiness outside of themselves*
- *often seeks love from people incapable of loving*
- *focus all your energy on another person's problems*
- *cover up and lie to protect loved one*

These habits tend to lead you into or keep you in unhealthy and destructive relationships. Codependency robs you of the freedom to live and enjoy life.

When I was faced with my husband's addiction, I was constantly afraid that he would relapse. I was literally obsessed with his addiction. I never knew when it was going to happen again, and I tried to control his behavior by picking up his check each pay day so he would not blow it all on drugs. I would not attend church functions without him for fear that if I left him alone at home he would leave while I was gone and use drugs. I slept with the keys to the car under my pillow fearing he would take the keys out of my purse and leave in the car while I was sleeping. I got involved in his rehab program, so I could learn everything about his addiction hoping I could stop him from using. I took responsibility for his negative behavior concerned for the consequences I would have to deal with otherwise.

I could not see that God was bigger than my situation. As a Christian woman, I believed it was my duty to just love him, support him and trust God to take care of it… but I was wrong. I realized that there were things God expected me to do and there were things God did not need me to do. There was nothing God could do as long as I was trying to control the situation and do His job for Him.

A woman's safety net is her home and when it is threatened, her natural instincts will kick into third gear and she will do whatever she has to do to feel safe and secure again.

Fear of abandonment and losing all we had, created such a conflict in me that I became attached to the situation on the one hand and detached from myself and God on the other. Pride led me to cover up and pretend everything was ok outwardly, while the enemy tormented me day and night with thoughts of my situation. I want to be clear, you will risk your financial stability if you continue bailing loved ones out of messes they created in order to keep others from knowing there is something wrong. Each time an item was taken from the house, I just replaced it and kept going. I began to lose sight of God's ability to handle the situation and I tried to take care of it myself. I lost touch of reality and my ability to think rationally and to feel. I had become obsessed with fixing the problem while losing Diane Parker (me), in the process. I lost my life, living it through the life of my husband. I enabled my husband to continue being irresponsible and unaccountable for his actions by not confronting his behavior and not allowing him to suffer the consequences of his actions.

As I laid prostrate before the Lord, I realized that I was not responsible for my husband's behavior. God did not create me to rescue or to become his savior or god. I realized that God was very capable of handling this situation if I would allow Him.

"I am so sorry Lord," I cried. *"I relinquish my need to be in control, to you. I give you all my fears. I cast the whole of my care on you because you care for me. Forgive me for not allowing you to be Lord in my life and over my circumstances. I ask you now to take control of my life and help me to see that are you bigger than my problems and pain. I receive your unconditional love for me. I receive your joy and peace in my life. I ask you to guide my steps. Show me how to walk faithfully in you. Help me to face my fears and turn them over to you. Thank you for your hand of mercy and grace over my life. I surrender my all to you now. In the name of Jesus, Amen."*

As I prayed I began to see God bigger than my circumstances. His love pierced through my pain and saturated my entire being. I began to sense His peace like never before. My heart and soul began to hunger and thirst for more of Him. "Lord I want to know you. Show me your face."

So do not fear, for I am with you; do not be dismayed, for I am your God. I will strengthen you and help you. I will uphold you with my righteous right hand. (Isaiah 41:10, NIV).

Chapter 6

Alone in His Presence

Seeking the Face and Heart of God

As I began to seek the face of God, I heard Him say in a quiet voice, "Diane, there is a place you can walk in Me and not be moved by anything going on around you. That is the place I want you to walk and live in Me. Your battle is designed to get you to that place." In my natural mind, I thought with all the hell going on around me, how can I not be affected by it, but deep within, I knew if God said it was possible, it was. If that is where He wanted me to be, I had to get there.

I felt an urgency within my spirit to begin to get up each morning at three a.m. to pray and fellowship with God. If I wanted to know Him, I would have to take the time to spend with Him daily. It was a sacrifice to interrupt my sleep and get up to pray, but I was desperate to know the heart of God. It was not enough to know of His blessings. I wanted to know the Giver of the blessings in a personal and intimate way. As I fellowshipped with the Lord each morning, I began to experience the stretching of my faith and the purging of my ungodly ways and thought patterns. I experienced the stripping of my pride, self-reliance and self-sufficiency. It was as if my skin was being peeled off, raw. The Lord began to purify my heart, burning out all that was not of Him through the power of the Holy Spirit. It was not His will for me to live carrying around all that baggage. He desired that I lived blessed and free.

The Secret Place

Once all the negative feelings and thoughts began to fade away, I was able to receive God's unconditional love for me. The death and resurrection of Jesus Christ became personal to me. Jesus died and rose for me that I might be free. The precious blood that Jesus shed as He was beaten was for my pain, transgressions and iniquity. He carried it on His back so I would not have to carry it or allow it to become bondage in my life. The Lord told me He would never leave me nor forsake me. I would never have to fear what man shall do to me (Hebrews 13:5&6). Then He reminded me that I was fearfully and wonderfully made (Psalm 139:14), and I was His work of art (Ephesians 2:10).

Each time He would whisper those words of affirmation into my spirit, He would direct me to the place where it was written in The Bible. Then I quietly asked, "Lord, how do I walk in a place where I am not moved by the storms in my life?" He led me to Psalms 91:1 (Amplified). As I read it, the words came alive to me. It reads, "He who dwells in the secret place of the Most High shall remain stable and fixed under the shadow of the Almighty (Whose power no foe can stand). I started to pray, breathe and live this verse. I understood that this was the place the Lord desired for me to live. In this *secret place,* I am at home in God. I have the privilege and comfort of knowing that under His shadow, He shelters me. I have residence there. This is my safe haven. I have become fully persuaded now that nothing can separate me from His love (Romans 8:38). I have serenity of mind because God is my resting place. He has become my home!

Healing Thought

I am with thee to deliver thee, saith the Lord.
(Jeremiah 1:8)

Chapter 7

Complete Forgiveness

*W*ebster's dictionary defines forgiveness as, to give up resentment against; stop being angry with; to give up all claim to punish or exact penalty for an offense; to overlook; to cancel or remit a debt. That is a lot to ask for when you have been betrayed or mentally and emotionally abused. Colossians 3:13 says, "Bear with each other and forgive whatever grievances you may have against each other. Forgive as the Lord forgave you." Jesus tells us in Matthew 6:14 (Amplified) that, "If we forgive people their trespasses (their reckless and willful sins, leaving them, letting them go and giving up resentment) your heavenly Father will forgive you of your trespasses."

In the early years of my husband's addiction I went through the motions of forgiving him, but I now know today that at that time I never really reached complete forgiveness. I just wanted to feel better so when he said, "I am sorry", I would attach a condition to his apology and move on until the next time. Each time I did this, I robbed myself of the freedom that the Lord desired me to have. I buried deeper and deeper the resentment and bitterness I felt towards my husband for all the pain and embarrassment he had put me through. There were times when I wanted to physically hurt him. I am thankful for the mercy and grace of God because during those crucial times He stopped me from taking vengeance into my own hands.

As I began to develop intimacy with God and fellowship with Him daily, I was able to face my own brokenness and weaknesses which opened my heart to start the process of complete forgiveness. To completely forgive involves the act of forgiving, facing the cost, accepting your losses and grieving your losses. When I saw myself, I was no longer able to focus my attention on his wrongdoings. I no longer needed to hold on to my resentment and bitterness as a way of punishing him or holding him hostage.

To forgive him would free me within and bring joy back into my life, but with a price.

The Cost of Forgiveness

By forgiving my husband, I not only had to let go of the outcomes that would come by releasing him and allowing him to make his own choices (even if his choices destroyed our marriage). I also had let go of the right to make things work out the way *I* wanted them to work out and release him to God. This is not easy when you have been in the habit of manipulating and controlling everything.

As the Lord began to teach me true forgiveness and take me through the process, the act of forgiving came much easier. The difficulty was accepting what had happened before and what was happening right then in my marriage and life. I was left with a feeling of emptiness, as if I was a big donut with a hole in the middle. Dealing with the obvious losses such as financial security and the ability to trust were both difficult. But what was more difficult was the not so obvious losses - the loss of my hopes and dreams, the loss of my credit worthiness, all the missed birthdays, holidays and anniversaries. Forgiving him meant I had to accept that I had lost these things and give up my right of making him pay for the pain he caused me.

Lost Dreams

Every woman has dreams of a happy fulfilling marriage and life, but when faced with overwhelming circumstances that rob you of your joy and peace, those dreams soon vanish. Your dreams are suddenly replaced with fear, anguish and despair. Just being able to make it through the day is a miracle. So often when we are faced with disappointments and failures in our lives, we try desperately to let go of those failures and move on, but to experience complete forgiveness and healing, you must take the time to grieve your losses. To grieve is to come to terms with your loss and allow yourself to experience the full range of emotions that are associated with it.

I began weeping one day as I realized how much I had lost. I cried out to God to fill the emptiness in my heart. I heard Him say in a still small voice,

"Diane, you have to give it all to me. I can't do anything with it if you are still holding on to it."

As I continued to sob I began to make a list of all that I had lost from the material things to my hopes, dreams, joy, peace, reputation, the wasted time spent worrying, the years of my life I put on hold trying to control everything around me to feel safe, etc. I took each item and cut out slips of paper. I went on my balcony and placed each sheet of paper in an iron pot and built an altar on my barbecue grill. I lit a fire and I raised my hands up to God. I prayed, "Lord these are all the things that I have lost. I give them all to you now. I give up my right to have anyone pay me back. I know you are able to give these things back to me if you so choose. I trust you. You know what is best."

When I called out each item one by one, I would feel the emptiness leave. Quietly I heard the Lord say to me, "I am El Roy, I see all. I am a God of recompense, I will repay." From that day to now, God has paid me back in so many ways it is overwhelming.

All the while as I walked through this process of forgiveness, I began to see my husband as God sees him. It enabled me to separate the man from his behavior and wrongdoings. I felt grief and sorrow for his soul and prayed God's mercy for him. I remembered my own life and my own need for mercy and grace. Most of all, I remembered the ultimate price and sacrifice Jesus paid on the cross for all our sins. I don't ever want to lose sight of the fact that we all need God's Grace.

Healing Thought

For if you forgive other people when they sin against you, your heavenly Father will also forgive you. (Matthew 6:14 NIV)

Chapter Eight

Identity Crisis

*M*any of us have childhood scars and wounds from old relationships that have never been dealt with. As long as they remain hidden, we will bring all of that old baggage into new relationships expecting things to be different. We may even feel that our loved ones are not there for us when we don't receive from them what we expect. Although we often don't want to admit it, what we really expect is to feel better about ourselves. We want to be fixed. We seek our value and worth in other people, in our jobs, church ministries, etc. We place intense pressure on those around us to prove their love for us, placing impossible demands upon them. It's like getting a fresh fix everyday just to maintain good feelings about ourselves.

Some of us even compromise our standards and put up with unacceptable behavior because we, ourselves, are suffering from an identity crisis. Our lives become enmeshed in the life of our mate to the point where we don't know who we are. I was one of these people. I didn't have a clue who I was. I didn't have a life. My life was entangled in my husband's life. If you were to ever ask me how I was doing I would say *"ok"* and begin talking about him. I was no longer in touch with my feelings. Being consumed with his addiction robbed me of my identity.

Who Am I?

When you don't know who you are in Christ, you tend to settle for whatever comes your way. You'll remain in unhealthy relationships, feeling that you don't deserve better as a result of shame and unworthiness. You will allow others to trample all over you filling your life with hopelessness and despair. I had knowledge and an understanding of who God was and the importance of allowing Him to work in my life, but I did not know who I was in Him.

When I started to study the scriptures and meditate on the Word of God regarding my identity, I began to value myself and my life.

Psalms 139:13-15 says, "For You created my innermost being; You knit me together in my mother's womb. I praise You because I am fearfully and wonderfully made; Your works are wonderful, I know that full well. My frame was not hidden from You when I was made in the secret place." God created me fearfully and wonderfully. His works are wonderful; therefore, I am a precious jewel in His sight. Ephesians 1:4 tells me that He chose me before the creation of the world, to be holy and blameless in His sight. In love, He predestined me to be adopted as His daughter through Jesus Christ in accordance with His pleasure and will. Because of Christ I am holy and blameless in the sight of God.

Healing Thought

To the praise of the glory of his grace, wherein
He hath made us accepted in the beloved.
(Ephesians 1:6)

Chapter 9

The Fiery Darts of Judgment

Standing on the outside looking in,
You freely voice your opinion and negative comments
Unsolicited, unwanted, unmerited,
Based on your thoughts, your personality,
what you believe, not fact
What is the purpose? What is there to gain?
A juicy conversation piece, joy in someone
else's failure or defeat!

You boldly proclaim what you wouldn't take;
what you wouldn't do
forgetting everyone has their season, next it
could be you.
How do you know anyway, you're still
standing on the outside
looking in, now behind a tree?
How can you judge me?
You're not me, you haven't walked in my shoes?

The Bible says to love and forgive and give unconditionally
You who are strong, bare the infirmities of the weak
It says you will have to give an account for
every idle word you speak.
You will reap what you sow,

Death and life are in the power of your tongue.
You will be judged the same way you judge me.
So, if I am wrong, pray for me
If I am weak, hold up my arms
But, how can you?
You are still standing on the outside looking in.
Could it be that if you stepped inside,
You would see a glimpse of you, in me?

One day after having several darts of judgement thrown at me, I sat down and wrote the poem above. I get so weary of having to deal with the sharp tongues, whispers, and unsolicited opinions of others. So-called Christians are usually the worst ones. Everybody has an opinion of what you should and should not do. Most them have never walked in your shoes and are quick to point fingers when someone's behavior does not fit into their box of reasoning or understanding. I am the first to admit that my husband had issues and I have suffered much pain and shame because of his behavior. Furthermore, the fact that he was a Christian man made it more overwhelming because everybody's eyes were on him. You see… drugs and sexual addictions are visible sins. The devastation and trauma they cause are exposed for all eyes to see. Yet in the sight of God these sins of the flesh are no different than the sins of lying, gossiping, jealousy, bitterness, resentment, etc.

I remember early on in his addiction I was complaining to the Lord about his behavior. Soon after, the Lord spoke to me and said, "Diane, who are you to judge him. You have not walked in his shoes. I gave you grace in your weakness. Man looks at the outward appearance, but I look at the heart. You just be his wife and let me be his God." I immediately repented. From that point on I have been very careful about passing judgment on my husband or for that matter, others. Even in his lying, deceit, betrayal, and breach of our marriage vows, God was still loving and forgiving. I realized even more the depth of God's love for His children. Romans 8:23 says, we all have sinned and come short of His glory. Strangely, God had allowed me to see my husband's heart for Him and that his path of destruction had a purpose bigger than I could ever imagine or think. Whether he chose to totally surrender to God and allow the healing to begin was between him and God. I had to make sure that I kept my side of the street clean.

Many have said to me, "I don't know how you do it. I don't know how you can still even talk to him and pray for him. There is no way I would put up with that!" It was not about putting up with it, it was learning to separate the man from the insane behavior. Just the emotional trauma alone was enough to give up. By knowing who I am and whose I am, I would not allow myself to be defined by what others thought of me. I was not validated by my husband or anyone else. My identity is in Christ. He is the Alpha and the Omega. He is the beginning and the end. I have learned to seek God in every decision I have made regarding my life's journey. I have listened to well-meaning friends who spoke things out of their emotions because they did not understand. I have heard the whispers behind my back while they are smiling in my face. I have watched the body language and seen the rolling eyes. I've seen the walking the other way to avoid crossing my path. Opinions mean nothing to me when it comes to seeing a loved one trapped in sin. It is our Christian duty to stand in the gap for those bound by life controlling problems, regardless of how it makes us feel.

I can count on one hand those who have said to me, "Diane, I may not understand it and I may not like it, but I am praying for you and I am standing with you for your loved one's deliverance."

Every day as I seek the face and heart of God, I am endeavoring to continue to walk in that place where I am not moved by what is going on around me. When the darts hit me, sometimes they bounce off and other times they sting. But even in those times I have a Comforter Who is there to comfort me and keep me. Hebrews 4:15 & 16 assures me that I do not have a high priest who is unable to sympathize with my weaknesses, but I have one who has been tempted in every way, just as I am, yet was without sin. Therefore, I can approach the throne of grace with confidence, so that I may receive mercy and find grace to help me in my time of need.

Healing Thought

When thou passeth through the waters, I will be with thee; and through the rivers, they shall not overflow thee; when thou walkest through the fire, thou shalt not be burned; neither shall the flame kindle upon thee. (Isaiah 43:2)

Chapter 10

Confronting My Fears

ever will I leave you. Never will I forsake you." So we say with confidence, "The Lord is my helper. I will not be afraid. What can man do to me?" These comforting words from Hebrews 13:5-6 became my saving grace. After a few weeks of meditating on this scripture I was faced with the test of living it. Did I really believe that God would never forsake me or leave me? Did I really believe that I don't have to be fearful of what man can do to me? Am I really ready to face the truth of how I had allowed my husband's behavior to take a toll on me emotionally? Am I ready to face the pain that was already beginning to develop into a rage I never knew possible? I had to come to grips with my husband's addiction and tell myself the truth regarding his behavior.

Telling myself the truth

What is the truth in this situation? My husband's behavior is his and I am not responsible for it. Yes, I needed to own my own frustration and anger but his choices were his choices alone. His behavior patterns were up and down. When he was in the cycle of his addiction it would last a week or a month at a time. He would go a while and not use or even look at pornography and then one day he would decide that he needed a break and he would begin using drugs and watching porn once again. If that day happened to fall on a Monday, then every Monday for the next month to six weeks he would act out. This would last until something terrible happened to bring him back to his senses.

You have to understand that addiction has a life of its own. It doesn't matter that you are involved in church. It doesn't matter that you break your marriage covenant. It doesn't matter that if you blow all the money, the bills would not get paid and you could lose everything.   It doesn't matter that one hit could prove deadly and your heart could stop. You lose all sense of reasoning and fulfilling your fleshly desires becomes most important.

What is the truth? It is a choice he decided to make.   In the world of drugs and pornography there are no boundaries.   You believe you have the right to take anything you want to take for your own pleasure. The property rights of others are ignored and if there is something you have that he needs to fulfill his fantasy he will take it.

What is the truth? He can only do to me what I allow. I allowed his behavior to rob me of life. Doing what is right does not mean that I jeopardize my life by giving up my peace and joy in exchange for the anxiety and anguish that came with these addictions. It meant I became responsible for my own things and would leave the rest. It meant that I could not force my will on the will of another.

What is the truth? What I become in the midst of my storm is not because of what happened to me, it is what I do with what happened to me. I remembered becoming fixed on a certain prayer that pulled down strongholds and broke bondages. I religiously and frantically prayed this prayer every day because I wanted the behavior to stop. When the prayer didn't work, I went to God in frustration and asked why. He told me that I was trying to manipulate my situation using scriptures over my husband. I could pray until I was blue in the face, but if he did not have the desire or will to change, he would remain in the same state.

What does the Word of God say about fear? II Timothy 1:7 says, "For God hath not given us a spirit of fear, but a spirit of power, love and a sound mind." First, fear is a spirit that does not come from God but from satan. Secondly when you don't deal with your fears they become strongholds in your life. My unresolved childhood issues of abandonment at a crucial moment in my life became an area of darkness in my life. My husband leaving me stranded at work and then taking off in the car one evening after I fell asleep, had emotionally traumatized me. It became even more real when my car broke down and I had no way to work. The dealership repairing my car told me they could not give me a loaner car so for a week I went without transportation, getting to work the best way I could. I began to meditate on Ephesians 4:27 where it says in Amplified Bible, "Leave no such room or foothold for the devil. Give no opportunity to him." I realized that I had given the devil a foothold in my life. He had every opportunity to torture me with fear because I had given him a place to live in my heart. It was at this point in my life that I made the decision that I was either going to stand on the Word of God and believe what it said or I would be miserable for the rest of my life. He said that He would never leave me nor forsake me (Hebrews 13:5).

When I began to submit this area of my life to God and apply all that I had learned up to this point, a light went on in my head. I yelled aloud, "I don't have to be afraid. God loves me and He will never leave me. It doesn't matter if my husband leaves me and never comes back, God will never leave me. He will always be there for me." Then I prayed, "God I give you all my fears. I choose to trust you. Replace my fear with your joy and peace." The love of God engulfed my entire being. It pierced through my pain and freed me. I felt a peace that I had never experienced. Miraculously, immediately after that prayer, the phone rang and it was the dealership. They had a car for me! My heart leaped with joy. Right then I heard the Lord say, "I told you I would not leave you nor forsake you." From that point, my life had changed. God had shown me in a very tangible way His unconditional love for me. I no longer had to fear being stranded or abandoned. No matter what I would face then or in the future, God was bigger than my situation and circumstances and I didn't have to be afraid any longer. What can man do to me?

Healing Thought

And ye shall know the truth and the truth shall make you free. (John 8:32)

Chapter 11

Confronting the Addiction

*W*e had been separated for nine months. Although my husband did not live in the house, he called me at least two or three times a week. There would be times when he would call every day for weeks at a time and then stop. It appeared from the outside that he was getting away with everything. There seemed to be no consequence for the things he did to indulge his fantasies and desires. Up to this point I had not really confronted his behavior in a way where he knew I was serious. I had allowed the traumatic effects of his addictions to rob me of my joy and strip me of the authority I knew I had over satan through Jesus Christ. I could not rise out of my despair. There were times I tolerated his behavior because I did not want to deal with all the drama that came when he did not get his way. It was as though he had developed a new skill by the manipulative stories he came up with. I learned that the mind of an addict easily becomes a slave of the drugs. He became an expert at lying his way out of things and manipulating to get whatever he needed to use.

Thankfully, I continued to fellowship with the Lord daily, learning His heart and seeking His direction every step of the way and I began to feel His power and strength working within me. I remember a specific time while I was at work, my husband had somehow gotten into my apartment. I came home to find that he had come in, taken a shower and helped himself to the refrigerator. You can imagine how fear tried to grip my soul. All I could think of was the items missing from the apartment. I called our family friend and asked that he come over and take my valuable items to his house. When I hung up I went into my prayer closet. At that moment, this thought struck me, what am I doing? Satan is not going to run me out of my house. I know who I am in Christ. I will not fear what man can do to me. I shouted in a loud voice, "devil you will not take anything out of this house and you will not torment me with fear and anxiety. The greater One lives within me (1 John 4:4). You will no longer have place in my life." I called our friend back and told him not to come that I was going to leave everything in place.

Thinking he may come back the next day, I left a note, "God loves you, surrender, you don't have to do this." I prayed over it and went to bed.

The next day, my husband came to the house again while I was at work but when he saw the note, he turned around and left. A few days later he came by claiming he wanted help. I agreed to go with him to meet with the director of the program he would later enroll in. It was a one year Christian program that was two hours away, designed to help people with life controlling problems develop discipline in their lives using God's biblical principles. Since he was leaving in a few days, I agreed to let him stay in the house. Two days before he was to leave, he decided to go out and use. He later called me and told me that he was feeling so depressed and sad about all he had done, it drove him to use. I immediately said to him, "no you are not depressed. You went out because you wanted to. This is just an excuse you are using to try and justify your actions but it does not work anymore. I love you but I am not buying into your excuses and lies anymore. You are out of control and you need help." Shocked at my response, he quietly said "You are right," and apologized. He entered the program and stayed a total of nine months.

Healing Thought

For I can do everything through Christ, who gives me strength. (Philippians 4:13, NLT)

Chapter 12

Broken - Discovering the Purpose of My Pain

*G*od has a way of using difficulties as tools to perfect specific areas in our lives. As I continued to learn of Him and His purpose for my life, I realized that He was using my circumstances to perfect me in those areas that would prepare me for a greater work for Him. God did not only want me well, He wanted me whole – spirit, soul and body. I needed to learn to trust God in every area of my life and not just those areas I wanted to give Him - every area.

Trust was a big issue in my life. It began as a child being sexually abused by a trusted family member. It progressed from there with disappointments, continuous let downs, and a misused and broken heart. All of us have been disappointed in our lives and we'll likely have disappointments as long as we are alive. The key is to work through your disappointments and failures and surrender them to God. I did not always do that. I allowed my being self-sufficient, self-reliant, and self-serving to make up for those times. I wore a mask to hide my insecurities and fears.

God knew all of the areas that I saw as a strength in my life and targeted those areas to bring me to a place of total dependence on Him. Between the two of us, my husband and I made good money. Unconsciously I began to depend on that money and looked at that as my source. I also was very proud of my credit because I had managed to build it up and keep a clean record.

When the addictions began to surface, my credit and our finances were the first things to go. When my husband began to blow his check and I could not pay the credit cards I fell apart because I lost sight of my true source. Moreover, I had never submitted my emotions to God. I trusted Him in every other area but when it came to opening up and really giving Him the hurt and pain I had suffered in my past, I kept that area under lock and key. It was no wonder that when my husband, the man I *finally* learned to trust, betrayed me, I was devastated. I was put in a situation where I could not run to anyone but God.

God desired to break me so He could put me back together. He began to shake everything in my life that hindered my relationship with Him.

He also began to expose old thinking patterns and behaviors that were not pleasing to Him. I had a choice, either submit to the shaking or run from it and prolong my breaking process. I desired God's best in my life so I submitted to His breaking process. Anything in our lives that hinders our relationship with God will be stripped away from us. It's not that He doesn't want us to have things, He doesn't want us to trust others or things more than Him. I studied and meditated on John 1:5 which says, "And the Light shines on in the darkness, for the darkness has never overpowered it (put it out or absorbed it, or appropriated it, and is unreceptive to it)." I began to ask God to shine His light of truth in the areas of darkness in my life. I learned that any area of darkness in my life would be revealed if I sincerely asked in faith. God also began to show me things about my husband that enabled me to understand some of what was happening in my life and why I was affected by it.

What we don't understand we judge. We lack compassion for others who may be struggling in areas that we are not struggling.

I began to take note of the things that continued to occur repeatedly, especially those things that affected me, and I realized that I still had not reached the point where I totally trusted God in certain areas. You see, I was still trying to control and save myself.

Healing Thought

---

*Not only so but we also glory in our sufferings,
because we know that suffering produces
perseverance; perseverance, character; and
character, hope. And hope does not put us to shame,
because God's love has been poured out into our
hearts through the Holy Spirit who has been given to
us. (Romans 5:3-5).*

Chapter 13

Picking Up the Pieces

Healing and Restoration

I remember many times feeling like I would never be free from the effects of my husband's addiction. I did not want to hurt anymore. As far as I was concerned, if it wasn't in my face then I did not have to deal with it. God wanted me to face my fears and my pain and understand that no matter what my husband was doing or anyone else, I needed to be okay in Him. I had confronted most of my fears and pain, but I was still reacting to the behavior.

---

*During my time of prayer and fellowship He
revealed to me that I had to be dead to it,
unmoved! Meaning, I had to become dead to his
behavior and all that comes with it.*

"How can I be dead to something when it is all in my face?" I

asked. By living and breathing Galatians 2:20, dying to yourself and

allowing Christ to live in you. I had to come to a place where I laid

it all at the feet of Jesus and left it there. I had to trust God to take

care of me no matter what. I had to believe by faith that He was big

enough to heal my broken heart and bind up my wounds (Psalms

147:3). Once I saw the big picture, I started to practice dying to

myself daily. Some days I lost, but I was determined to not allow my

emotions to dictate how my day would be. As I died to my flesh

daily, Christ became more alive and began to live big within me.

Throughout our marriage, I never dishonored or disrespected

my husband. I did not put him down nor was I mean or nasty. I was

firm and I continued to walk in love even when my flesh was

screaming to retaliate. During a pretty peaceful period of our lives, my husband and I decided to move to Florida. We prayed about it and a door opened. He was convinced all we needed was a new start and everything would be fine. Wrong! Within five weeks the behavior started again. I saw the behavior changes and warned him but he did not listen to me. Determined that I was not going to tolerate it, I told him if he did it again he would have to leave. Defiant, he made up his mind to do what he wanted to do, not taking me seriously and went out again the next week. I knew in my heart this was it. I packed his bags and sent him back to Texas.

What I didn't realize was God had a purpose in this also. I had reached a level of trust in God where I was no longer moved by his behavior. My husband's behavior no longer would be in my face. God would not use it as tool for that particular area of my life. God moved him. He could no longer just do whatever he wanted to do at any cost and then run back home. He was now over 1,000 miles away. He would have to see the ugly in himself and face his own demons.

He admitted, "When you stood up to me by not being moved by my behavior, I had to go around you and when I did, I had to face God." Shocked and angry at my response to his behavior, my husband fell deeper into sin in his rebellion against God. From the moment he turned his back on everything he knew to be right and acted contrary to the Word of God, he was about to face a huge consequence, something that had not happened up to this point.

For the next few weeks I had to take the time to work through my anger and feelings of being hurt and left alone. I was in a strange town. I was left again to pick up the pieces. As I spent time before the Lord, He gave me the grace to forgive my husband and to grieve my loss. I wanted to just write him off and never have anything else to do with him. My flesh told me, "Ok this is it. I don't have to deal with him anymore." Straightaway the Lord rebuked me and said these words, "I moved him, but I did not tell you to divorce him. He is still your husband. If you are faithful and will lay down your life in prayer for him, I will turn your whole life around." I was upset and wanted to have a pity party, so I continued waddling in my anger. After about a week of feeling sorry for myself the Lord spoke to me again and told me to begin laying my life down in prayer for my husband. He said, "You have been praying for him out of your pain not as My son. I love him just as much as I love you. He needs someone committed to praying for him to save his life." Honestly, I don't know how I responded except to say, "Lord, You will have to teach me."

A few days later I walked into a store and there in front of me was a display of Christian books. As I began to look through the books, *The Power of a Praying Wife*, by Stormie Ormartian caught my attention. I heard the Lord say, "Get that book!" So I purchased it and went home.

From the moment, I read the first chapter I was overwhelmed with tears. Here I was, reading some of the very same things that the Lord had previously spoken to my heart. I knew at that point my life would never be the same. God's purpose and plan began to become more real to me. He began to teach me how to pray for my husband as well as His best for him and in doing so I began to see him differently.

One morning while praying the Lord showed me a vision of my husband walking and then disappearing into air. He said that he had totally given over to the drug scene. For the next several months I prayed specific prayers for my husband as the Holy Spirit led. I did not know where he was, but I heard through a friend that he was living on the streets and in a crack house. I had been praying for him about three months when one night the Lord spoke to me and told me to speak to my husband's spirit because that was the only part of him that satan did not have. As I began to obey the voice of God I sensed my husband's heart crying out for help. I prayed all night. Two days later the phone rang and it was him. He said that he had been living on the streets and was using drugs every day. He recounted how he had gotten to a place where he desperately wanted to get out but felt helpless to do so. Then he heard someone calling him and he was able to get enough strength to get up from where he was and walk away. He went to his sister's house and asked her if he could use her phone to call me. It was actually during the same time the Lord instructed me to speak to his spirit. He reached out for help and entered into another rehab center.

I witnessed God strategically move in my circumstances and my faith soared. My trust in Him reached a level I had never experienced. There was no doubt in my mind that He had my back and that He would see me through whatever I faced. I had learned to trust Him with my heart issues as I sought to learn His heart. It was at this point in my life that I began to feel his healing power saturate my entire being, making me whole.

It was as though I was a broken vase being put back together again.

I learned that a big part of inner healing is dying to yourself. Healing doesn't erase a memory or change our history, but it enables us to cherish the worst moments. It is through those moments God can inscribed eternal lessons onto our lives so we're able to minister to others who have suffered in the same way we have. Finally, … I was being made whole again. I knew who I was in Christ and who He is by studying His Word and spending quality time in fellowship and prayer. Through making a daily decision to surrender to God, Christ was able to live within me flushing out my pain, fears and insecurities. My soul has been restored (Psalms 23:3).

I have relinquished my false sense of security. I no longer control others to fulfill a need within. I now trust Him who is the "Keeper of my Soul." Learning how to pray God's best for my husband and seeing him as a son of God first and foremost, then as my husband, has also brought healing to my soul. I was no longer bound by bitterness and anger. In His presence, I found healing and restoration.

Healing Thought

---

*For I will restore health to you, and your wounds
I will heal, declares the Lord. Jeremiah 30:17
(ESV)*

Chapter 14

The Final Breaking

The next few years would prove to be challenging but I was in a different place spiritually so I knew what to do when fear tried to rob me of my faith and trust in God. My husband had returned to Florida and was making an effort to live a better life. I had three major surgeries which brought added stress and behavior issues. During this time, my husband found himself slipping back into his old behaviors.

I knew that if a person is not rooted and grounded in the Word of God, connecting with Him daily, that person would soon find themselves engulfed and consumed in sin again. As a result, I had to enforce tougher boundaries that would force my husband to face himself and the depth of his addictions. In the middle of all of this, I was suddenly laid off from my job. Three months later, I found another job. Two weeks later, my husband made the decision to go back into a Christian Rehabilitation Ministry Center for restoration. I was angry and disappointed. Not only were we down to one income but I made considerably less than what I previously made and it put a tremendous strain on me. Old thoughts of resentment and feelings of abandonment tried to peak its ugly head.

I did not know how I would make it from week to week. Everything I learned would be put to a test but I realized it was another opportunity to stretch my faith and trust in God.

The Word of God is true, and it is important that we take heed in every area of our lives. There are promises of life and blessings but also a warning of what happens when we become comfortable and are no longer alert and spiritually watchful in our walk with God. 1 Peter 5: 8 declares, "Be alert and of sober mind.

Your enemy the devil prowls around like a roaring lion looking for someone to devour." According to Luke 11:24-26, "When an impure spirit comes out of a person, it goes through arid places seeking rest and does not find it. Then it says, 'I will return to the house I left'. When it arrives, it finds the house swept clean and put in order. Then it goes and take seven other spirits more wicked than itself, and they go in and live there. And the final condition of that person is worse than the first." (NIV) This Word of God illustration of what happens when an unclean spirit returns would soon become a reality in my husband's life. I would again face another storm. This time not only was the door blown off the hinges, but the roof blew off as well. It was in this new season, I would truly learn how to walk in the power, strength and grace of God.

My husband went into the Center determined to change. He received major deliverance, surrendered to God and submitted to the call on his life. He entered a leadership program and also became a certified biblical counselor. He was hired by the ministry and began working with the students that entered the program. He felt good about his accomplishments and was happy to be drug free and walking in his purpose.

Meanwhile, I worked through my disappointment and surrendered to the stretching and testing of my faith. I stood, I prayed, I cried and prayed and cried some more, remaining faithful to the call of 'wifehood'. We talked on a regular basis, but emotionally I was still trying to find my way through the losses I recently experienced. After a while, I began to notice a change in his conversation. He became restless and started complaining about feeling stuck, unable to do other things. I began praying for him asking God to reveal what was really going on. The Lord revealed that there was another level of healing and deliverance my husband needed to go through to deal with the root cause of his addiction. But, if he was not careful or did not recognize what he was feeling was a distraction from the enemy, he would be drawn away by his own lust (James 1:14).

I remembered my husband sharing about his childhood pain and how over the years he had learned to cope. Whenever he felt stressed, overwhelmed or rejected, he would turn to pornography and drugs. It was in this place of restlessness where he would seek attention and a way to fulfill his longings. Since he never allowed God to heal the root of rejection and feelings of low self-esteem and failure, he surrounded himself with people who stroked his ego and gave him whatever he wanted without any questions.

I tried repeatedly to warn him that he was being distracted and satan was setting him up to pull him off course. He did not listen and became very arrogant and high-minded. He began to say he felt like he was missing a part of his life. He believed that because his behavior had improved now, and he was in a better place, he was ready to go back to Dallas to be with his family. I thought to myself:

I have walked with you all this time, stood by your side, labored in prayer for your soul, cried, cleaned your messes, experienced financial loss and now that you are better, you want to go back to Dallas? I was there when no one else was there. I stayed when everyone else walked away. I prayed for this moment; you walking in your purpose, drug-free, living life together and you want to leave?

I was crushed. My heart was broken. A week later, I received a call from him. He had left the ministry, and was on his way home. Although he said he was home to save his marriage, truth be told, he had made a decision to go back to Dallas and nothing was going to stop him. He wanted to prove to everyone he was not a failure and was proud of what he had accomplished. I remember crying out to God asking for His direction in this situation. He answered, "Let him go. Leave it alone. You can't save him or protect him." I retreated to my quiet place and allowed the Holy Spirit to comfort my spirit and bring peace to my soul. A few days later he headed back to Dallas.

Happy to be free to do whatever he wanted with no accountability, my husband eventually became entangled with sin again - this time on a much larger level. Satan had successfully enticed him to walk away from his call, ministry, and marriage. Just as the scripture states, when the spirit finds the house empty, he brings seven more spirits and the person finds himself in worse condition than the first.

Think of it this way... you've been instructed by your physician to take medication for your illness. He specifically tells you to take all the medication. You start out focused because the pain is seemingly unbearable. But as time goes you start feeling better and neglect to finish the dosage as instructed. Before you know it you're sicker than you were before. I would soon learn that because he chose this path for his life, the Lord allowed him to leave so He could do a greater work in my life without the pain and distractions.

My husband was not 'better'. He simply stopped abusing drugs without dealing with the root cause of his addiction. As long as he made those choices, he found himself in a worse state than before. Truth is, he needed another level of healing but he chose to walk away from that place of safety where he could receive his healing. Sadly, he would have to struggle daily just to receive that healing and it was all because he chose this road. It was not until I took responsibility for my part and released my disappointment and anger to God that He revealed this truth. I no longer felt I had missed out on something. Instead I embraced the path that would lead me to God's next dimension in my life.

Healing Thought

No, in all these things we are more than conquerors through him that loved us. (Romans 8:37)

Chapter 15

Taking Back My Life

I have learned that life is a precious gift from God and getting bogged down with 'stuff' will cause you to miss living.

---

*M*y husband was responsible for his own behavior and would suffer the consequences of his decisions. It was time for me to live and enjoy the life God had given me. You see, dear friend, God does not desire that we live our lives bogged down with 'stuff'. He wants us to give the 'stuff' to Him. 1Peter 5:7 (Amplified), "Cast the whole of your cares on Him for He cares for you."

Prior to being broken before the Lord, I thought I had it going on. I was deceived. I had my scriptures that I would stand on and quote on a regular basis. I read my Bible faithfully and prayed several times a day. I was involved in church. I had my circle of friends. I ran around in my god suit on trying to save the world. What I thought was living was actually bondage. I was not living. I had only been existing. I had moments of happiness but I did not have true joy in my life.

I was missing the one ingredient that brings true joy in your life and that is intimacy and fellowship with God. It's having a one on one relationship and surrendering every area of my life to Him. It's one thing to know about God and to be able to quote the scriptures but it's another thing to spend quality time communing with Him regularly; getting to know Him for who He is and becoming one in Him. It is just like a couple who has been married a long time and has allowed God to transform them. They become like each other. Sometimes they finish each other's sentences because they are of one mind and one heart. Their love for each other fills them with joy, peace, gentleness and faithfulness.

Once I became one with God, my surrendered heart found joy in Him. I experienced and continue to experience the awesomeness and power of God's love for me. I learned that when you truly grasp God's love, joy is the response to the presence of God's love in your soul. When we learn to relinquish our lives to God and look to Him as our source, we become transformed. We don't look at life in the same way. We don't worry about the things that happen to us or around us. We don't try to find happiness in other people, our jobs or things. Joy is not a result of seeking after joy, it is a result of seeking after the Lord. The more we learn of God's love for us, the more we desire to love Him with all our heart, soul and strength (Deut. 6:5). When we rid ourselves of our inflated egos and our need to be in control we find ourselves filled with glorious abundant joy.

A surrendered life to God brings the freedom to live. Don't get me wrong, you'll still have problems and you're sure to be challenged by life's struggles, but the good news is now you are one with Him, and you won't ever have to be confused about Who is in charge. Even better, you no longer have to carry the weight of the world on your shoulders. By regaining my life, I took the following steps and to this day I continue to follow them in my life.

Admit that I had been playing god in the lives of others

I had to face the fact that I don't have the power nor the strength to save and rescue others. Many of our loved ones cannot receive the breakthroughs in their lives because we often get in the way by trying to protect them from themselves. Trying to control everyone and everything around us is a defense mechanism used to keep us from looking at ourselves. We don't want to face our own fears and pain. Unfortunately, in doing that, you rob yourself of the ability to live a healthy fruitful life. As long as you hide behind the lives of others or live your life through the lives of others, you will not grow, instead you will remain emotionally bankrupt. You will always find yourself in the middle of someone else's mess allowing satan (the enemy of our souls) to keep you in that rut. You may experience moments of happiness but inevitably, you will never experience the joy of true freedom and wholeness in God.

Spend quality time in fellowship and prayer with God

I had to learn who I am in Christ and who He is in me by studying His word. The more I spent time with the Lord, the more I developed an intimate relationship with Him. By getting to know Him, my confidence, faith and trust in Him enabled me to let go of my fears and insecurities. Thankfully, when I feel the world is closing in on me, I would remember what Jesus did during such times. He would slip away and find a place to pray. In my time of prayer, I am able to see God *bigger* than my problems and circumstances and I trust Him completely to work it out.

Guard my heart

Proverbs 4:23 says, "Guard your heart above all else, for it determines the course of your life." Our heart is our affections, desires and impulses. We are commanded to guard it because it determines every outcome of our life. It is the command center.

What we say and do, does not come from outward influences, but it flows from within. The enemy, satan, targets our heart. If he can derail our hearts by affecting our impulses, desires and affections, he can wreck our lives. As I allow the Word of God to penetrate deep within my soul, my heart is protected and guarded. Then, and I mean only then, am I able to make decisions based on the Word and will of God…not what my flesh desires.

Silence the voice of outside influences

It seems that when we feel we have been wronged, hurt or disappointed we want others to hear our pain and agree with us about the wrong we have experienced. The bottom line is we want them to comfort our souls. Early on, I was guilty of this but it only intensified the enemy's involvement in my thoughts and hindered the work of grace and mercy in my life. Furthermore, I received the un-solicited opinions of others about what I should and should not do. I got to the point where I knew that the only way to clearly hear God's voice as He directed my steps, was to stop allowing any and everyone to talk to me about my husband or my current situation.

At the same time, that also meant *I* would have to stop sharing the intimate details of our struggles.

Sever ungodly soul ties

The soul consists of the mind, will and emotions. According to Dictionary.com, to 'tie' means to bind, fasten, attach, secure, link, cleave. In my marriage, my husband and I became tied as one. An ungodly soul tie will cause you to experience and be affected by the will, the mind, the emotions, and the spiritual condition of the person with whom you are connected. His behavior not only caused me to shut down emotionally, there were times when he was able to manipulate me to get what he wanted to feed his habit. My soul was also tied to fear, distrust, negativity and pain as a result. Severing these soul ties brought healing and restoration to my soul. I was able to finally discern between manipulation and truth.

Set boundaries

I no longer do for others what they can do for themselves. I allow others to take responsibility for their own actions and suffer their own consequences for negative behavior. I do not allow others to define who I am. I am responsible for my own wellbeing. I say no when I mean no. I don't over commit myself or continue to give when it is emotionally or physically unhealthy. I have separated myself from negative people and I am now making room for joy in my life.

Celebrate yourself

Take time out for yourself. As a wife and/or a mother you are still a woman who has needs that have to be met. Physically, get the proper nutrition, exercise, get plenty of rest and practice proper hygiene. Mentally, stimulate your intellect by reading and learning. Emotionally, take the time to allow to 'exhale' and to express your emotions as they relate to your everyday life. Intimately connect with others. Spiritually, feed your spirit by spending time in prayer and quiet time with God by meditating on His word. He is your source of strength and power. See yourself as valuable and special. You are a unique gift from God.

Healing Thought

---

*Beloved, I wish above all things that thou mayest
prosper and be in health, even as thy soul
prospereth. (3 John 2)*

Chapter 16

Heels with Power

Moving forward from Here

*W*hen you come to the end of yourself, you reach a breaking point. There, you will find God standing with open arms to love you, comfort you, teach you and guide you. Recovering from this latest incidence was not an easy task, but I knew I had to move forward and allow God to heal my broken heart.

I had to own that it was my choice to stay and stand with my husband through the years of every roller coaster ride of his addiction.

I had to own that I was not always emotionally available to him because I was stuck in my own pain and disappointment. Once I took responsibility for *my behavior* and choices I was able to move forward and experience the place of grace, peace and power in Christ.

In Chapter five, I shared how God told me there was a place in Him I could walk and not be moved by what is going on around me. Over the course of this journey, I realized that although, as a believer, I had authority in Christ (which is my position), it was necessary to align myself (which is my posture) with His Truth in order to walk in His power. This place is my relationship with Him. This place is abiding in Him and He abiding in me (John 15: 3-7). This place is being plugged into Him is where my real power source resides.

This place is allowing the Holy Spirit to be my ***Comforter*** and allowing Him to impact my life as ***Teacher***. "But the Counselor, the Holy Spirit, whom the Father will send in my name, will teach you all things and will remind you of everything I have said to you." John 14:26 (CEV). This place is where He is my ***Peace***. John 14:27 (NIV) states, "Peace I leave with you; *my peace* I give you. I do not give to you as the world gives. Do not let your hearts be troubled and do not be afraid."

This place is also knowing who the real enemy of my soul is (satan), and not being ignorant of his devices. 1 Peter 5:8 says "Be alert and of sober mind. Your enemy the devil prowls around like a roaring lion looking for someone to devour." Jesus conquered him when He died and rose from the grave. It's because I am in him, that I have been given that same authority. Luke 10:19 tells us, "Behold, I give unto **you** power to tread on serpents and scorpions, and over all the power of the enemy: and nothing shall by any means hurt you." In the secret place of the Most High God (Psalms 91), I found rest, peace, safety, power, grace and strength through living a life of prayer, praise and studying God's Word. He had *already* given me the tools when I accepted Jesus into my heart. I just needed to apply them to my life!

The power of God is released in my life through **prayer, praise, studying His word** and **applying it to my life**. Here are some of powerful nuggets I've learned to apply to my life for victory.

Prayer

- As I pray to God, He will answer me and reveal to me what I don't know.

Jeremiah 33:3 "Call unto me, and I will answer thee, and shew thee great and mighty things, which thou knowest not."

- As I pray in faith and in harmony with His will I can speak to mountains in my life to be removed.

- My faith along with God's power can produce amazing results in my life.

I assure you and most solemnly say to you, whoever says to this mountain, 'Be lifted up and thrown into the sea!' and does not doubt in his heart [in God's unlimited power], but believes that what he says is going to take place, it will be done for him [in accordance with God's will].
Mark 11:23 (AMP Version)

Praise

- Praise must become a lifestyle for us,

  I will bless the Lord at all times: His praise shall continually be in my mouth. (Psalms 34:1)

- He dwells in the atmosphere of my praise to Him.

  God inhabits the praises of his people. (Psalms 22:3)

- My praise is a vehicle of faith which takes me into His presence and power.

Studying God's Word

- As I study the word of God and apply it to my life, I do not have to live a defeated life. **There *is* power in the Word of God**.

  Ephesians 6:10-18. Finally, be strong in the Lord and in his mighty power. We are to be strong in the Lord and His power, not our own.

  ¹¹ Put on the full armor of God, so that you can take your stand against the devil's schemes. We are to put on the full armor of God, so we are

*able to stand in the midst of adversity. It protects
us and give us the power to stand against the
attacks of the enemy.*

*¹²For our struggle is not against flesh and
blood, but against the rulers, against the
authorities, against the powers of this dark world
and against the spiritual forces of evil in the
heavenly realms.*

**(Remember our battle is not with our husbands or wives,
family members and friends. Our battle is with the
demonic forces of satan and in this world influencing the
lives of our loved ones).**

*¹³Therefore put on the full armor of God, so that
when the day of evil comes, you may be able to
stand your ground, and after you have done
everything, to stand.*

*¹⁴Stand firm then, with the belt of truth buckled
around your waist, - knowing the truth of God's
word and allowing His truth to change us from
the inside out with the breastplate of
righteousness in place,*

*¹⁵and with your feet fitted with the readiness that
comes from the gospel of peace.*

*¹⁶In addition to all this, take up the shield of
faith, with which you can extinguish all the
flaming arrows of the evil one.*

¹⁷Take the helmet of salvation and the sword of the Spirit, which is the Word of God. "Praying always with all prayer and supplication in the Spirit.

Wearing the armor of God, gives me spiritual authority against Satan's attempts to attack me with discouragement, disappointment, pride, envy, doubt, fear, etc.

- Although satan is the god of this world, the power that is in me is greater than the power of the world. I can walk in the power and grace of God, knowing that I have the victory.

---

1 John 4:4 says, Ye are of God, little children and have overcome them in the world: because greater is He that is in you, than he that is in the world.

When I began this journey several years ago, I did not know where it would lead me. Blindly, out of obedience I took God's hand and surrendered my will, my emotions, my mind, my intellect, my life to Him, to do whatever He wanted.

---

*There were times when I couldn't even see past
my two feet but I knew as long as God had my
hand, everything would be alright.*

One day, while in prayer I asked Him why was I chosen to walk this particular path? He replied, "I knew I could trust you with pain. I knew you wouldn't bail out on Me and stop serving me when it got tough. I could trust you to stand in the gap for your husband and not waiver when no one else would. I could trust you to hold your peace in the midst of the fiery darts of judgment shot at you on a regular basis. I could trust you to obey Me no matter what it looked like to your natural eye." Then He took me to Psalms 25:14 where it says, "Friendship with the Lord is reserved for those who fear Him. With them He shows the secrets of His covenant." He said, "To fear Me is to believe Me. To believe Me is to obey Me. Now I call you friend." I had taken the time to get to know Him as I would a natural friend. As a result, just as a natural friend, He began to reveal to me the intentions and desires of His heart in my life and the lives of those around me.

I now understood why when something happened in my life or in the life of my husband, I was able to see past what was the obvious, glaring in my face. I understood that even if the devil brought it, God allowed it for a higher purpose. The sooner I submitted to His purpose, He showed me how to handle a situation before it transpired. I now understood even more, His unconditional love for me and His desire for His best in my life.

Out of my brokenness I have gained an understanding of God's unlimited grace. As I trust Him, the power of His grace is released in my life. I have a greater compassion for others and realize that we all need God's grace and the power of the Holy Spirit at work in our lives. Just as God was patient with me, I can be patient with others. Just as God has extended His grace and mercy to me, I can extend grace and mercy to others. Just as He forgave me, I can forgive those who hurt me.

God is sovereign. He is omnipotent. He is omnipresent. He knows all. He sees all. He is Alpha and Omega, the Beginning and the End. Isaiah 55:8-9, (Living Bible) declares, "This plan of Mine is not what you would work out, neither are My thoughts the same as yours. For just as the heavens are higher than the earth, so are My ways higher than yours and My thoughts than yours." God knows what is best for our lives. His ways are not our ways and His thoughts are not our thoughts.

He loves us so much that He sent His Son Jesus to die that we might be free in every area of our lives. "Surely, He has borne our grief's (sicknesses, weaknesses, and distresses) and carried our sorrows and pains (of punishment). But He was wounded for our transgressions, He was bruised for our guilt and iniquities; the chastisement (needful to obtain) peace and well-being for us was upon Him, and with the stripes (that wounded) Him we are healed and made whole," (Isaiah 53:4-5, Amplified). We don't have to walk this road alone. God is with us. He is El Shaddai, He is more than enough!

My journey was painful and at times and heart wrenching,

but the blessings of peace and intimacy with God I discovered, are priceless. I found that you can't have a true relationship with God and not change. The power of His love and presence refines you and burns everything out of you that is not of Him. Every day He shows me, me. He doesn't beat me over the head with it or condemn me or put me down. He doesn't broadcast my faults and shortcomings. He gently tells me and by His spirit He leads me, guides me and teaches me. At no time in my journey did I have to maneuver, manipulate or demand my own way. God strategically moved on my behalf.

He told me early on, "You be his wife and let me be His God", and I did just that. God did the moving and the shaking. I just obeyed His voice.

I remember God saying to me one day during a crying moment, "If you lay your life down in prayer for your husband, I will turn your whole life around." At the time, I thought it meant He would turn my marriage around and all would be well. Instead, the key word here is "your" meaning He was aiming to turn *my* life around. I missed that perhaps because I was desperate for the pain to stop. However, as I look back at while I was praying for my husband as God's son, He has completely turned my life around. I have joy and peace that I never knew possible. Job 42:10 says, "And the Lord turned the captivity of Job when he prayed for his friends." When Job began to step out of feeling sorry for himself and began lovingly praying for his friends, God delivered him out of his affliction.

I continue to daily commune with God, especially seeking His will and purpose for my life. It is not always easy because those old thinking patterns and behaviors try to reappear when trouble strikes, but I know who I am in Christ and I know that He will never leave me nor forsake me. God will not allow anymore on you than the grace He gives you to walk through it. As you begin your journey to freedom, you may experience moments of fear as you learn who you really are. But do not be afraid. God is faithful and He will never let you down. Once you experience His joy, peace and freedom you will never want to go back. His love for you is

powerful enough to pierce through your pain and fears and make

you whole. It will put a smile on your face and a song in your heart.

It will bring clarification and revelation of how to truly live in Him.

Healing Thought

---

*Trust in and rely confidently on the LORD with all
your heart and do not rely on your own
insight or understanding. In all your ways
know and acknowledge and recognize Him, and
He will make your paths straight and smooth
[removing obstacles that block your way].*
(Proverbs 3:5-6, AMP)

Chapter 17

Healing for those Affected by Addiction

*L*ife with someone with an addiction can be a very traumatic experience. The devastation of severe monetary loss, deceit, broken promises and dreams along with feelings of betrayal and mental anguish, even fear at times, can seem unbearable. Embarrassment and shame can overtake you.

The hopelessness and despair you feel may be indescribable, but there is hope. You can get through it. Your loved one may never change but you can.

The most important thing is to know that God has not left

you. He knows right where you are. Call on Him. Seek Him. Allow Him into the dark area of pain in your heart. Decide that you will no longer take on a victim mentality or feel defeated and powerless. If you put your hand in His hand, He will see you through to the other side. Just as Peter was able to walk on the water as long as he kept his eyes on Jesus and his hand in His hand, it will be the same for you. It wasn't until he focused on the waves that he began to sink (Matthew 14:28-30). If you remain focused on your pain and disappointments or your loved one's destructive behavior you will sink. Alternatively, while keeping your eyes on Jesus, your faith will be strong and remain strong. Praise be to God!!

.

The Healing Process

The following steps can help you get through the healing process:

- *Move beyond denial and admit there is a problem. Acknowledge how you are being affected. Be honest with yourself and God about how you feel.*
- *God desires to meet you at the center of your pain. Allow Him in. No matter how deep it is, He can reach you. Allow Him to meet your greatest need.*

- *Take responsibility for your life. Recognize your own areas of sin and brokenness and deal with it.*
- *Gain knowledge of the addiction.*
- *Stop being an enabler by keeping your loved one's secrets or hiding his or her addiction. Refuse to take responsibility for their behavior. Reject the lies and manipulation. You are not responsible for your loved one's choices. You are only responsible for your obedience to God's word.*
- *Remove all outside negative influences.*
- *Forgive even if you don't forget.*
- *Grieve your losses.*
- *Set boundaries.*
- *Pray for your loved one and release him or her to God. He is the only One Who can heal your loved one but it will only happen if they want it and are willing to do the work.*
- *Let your hope and happiness be found in the God of hope, not in your loved one's choices.*
- *Seek God's direction for your life and live.*

Epilogue

One of the most impactful blessings I have received on this journey is living, walking and breathing God's grace and healing power. To have experienced the depth of pain I have felt and yet when prompted by the Holy Spirit, to be able to minister and pray with a pure heart for a man who succumbed to his demons and walked away from everything, including our marriage, is indeed a miracle. I remember the day when the Lord said to me, "it is time to tell him you forgive him and release him from the debt you feel he owes you". Although I had finally reached a place of forgiveness, I was not ready to say the words out loud. However, God knew the impact. His timing is perfect. My husband was very shaken and humbled, for he knew all that he had done and continued doing at the time.

Witnessing the healing that had taken place in my heart despite all he had done, and having the ability to forgive him, caused him to experience God's unconditional love for him in a very tangible way, even in the midst of his rebellion and disobedience. He saw how much it was God's desire to heal him and free him from the core of his being. He was aware of God's love but it wasn't until I said the words, "I forgive you" that he realized God's love for him specifically, including the power of His mercy and grace.

Today I understand that my life's walk is a testament of God's grace, forgiveness and power. I am reaping the benefits and blessings of surrender. I have the awesome privilege of sharing the unconditional love of God with others, one on one, in group meetings, workshops, retreats and conferences, empowering them to turn their pain into power by applying the biblical truths of God's

Word in every situation they encounter. I have been *Processed into My Purpose.*

As of the writing of this book, my husband and I remain separated, but still communicate regularly. He has had several challenges but has finally reached a place of brokenness and has committed himself to God's healing, restoration and plan for his life.

As I look back I thank God for His process of brokenness. He allowed circumstances to shake my life and expose everything that was hindering His will and purpose for me. In surrendering every part of my being to Him, *I gave God me.* In return not only have I received His strength, grace and power for my journey but an abundance of peace, favor and emotional freedom I never knew possible. I see His hand day to day covering and protecting me from people, situations and circumstances that would have caused unnecessary drama and stress. I don't have to worry or fret because He has my back. My steps are ordered by Him.

I still have difficulties that I face but they no longer have

me. I run to that secret place where I find peace, rest and comfort for

my soul. Beloved, there is a blessing in surrender. May you find that

place as well.

1 Peter 5: 6-10 (Amplified) says:

> "*⁶Therefore humble yourselves under the mighty hand of God [set aside self-righteous pride], so that He may exalt you [to a place of honor in His service] at the appropriate time,*
>
> *⁷casting all your cares [all your anxieties, all your worries, and all your concerns, once and for all] on Him, for He cares about you [with deepest affection, and watches over you very carefully].*
>
> *⁸Be sober [well balanced and self-disciplined], be alert and cautious at all times. That enemy of yours, the devil, prowls around like a roaring lion [fiercely hungry], seeking someone to devour*
>
> *⁹But resist him, be firm in your faith [against His attack—rooted, established, immovable], knowing that the same experiences of suffering are being experienced by your brothers and sisters throughout the world. [You do not suffer alone.]*

*¹⁰After you have suffered for a little while, the
God of all grace [who imparts His blessing and
favor], who called you to His own eternal glory
in Christ, will Himself complete, confirm,
strengthen, and establish you [making you what
you ought to be."*

As you humble yourself before God, casting all your worries, anxieties and concern on Him, staying alert and sober of mind, resisting the devil, remaining firm in your faith, the God of all grace, will complete, strengthen, confirm and establish (settle) you. He cares about you. He desires you to be healed and whole, spirit, soul and body. Let Him restore your heart and reveal His amazing unconditional love for you. In Him you will find strength, power and grace for the journey!

Heels with Power

About the Author

Diane Parker is a Christian Counselor/Mentor, Ordained Minister of Pastoral Care, Inspirational Teacher and Speaker. She is a member of the American Association of Christian Counselors and the Addiction & Recovery Network. She is the founder of Women of Strength & Dignity Ministries; a ministry of inner healing, inspiration, restoration and strength. She has dedicated her life to helping others from all walks of life to turn their pain into power enabling them to stand in the midst of adversity with dignity, respect and faith in God. She resides in Orlando, FL where she serves as one of the Assistant Pastors at a local church.

TO PUBLISH YOUR
STORY OR BOOK

CONTACT

WILLIAMS & KING PUBLISHERS
888-645-0550
Info@WilliamsAndKingPublishers.com

OR

TO LEARN ABOUT
OTHER BOOKS
PUBLISHED BY

WILLIAMS & KING PUBLISHERS

VISIT

WilliamsAndKingPublishers.com

Notes

www.ingramcontent.com/pod-product-compliance
Lightning Source LLC
Chambersburg PA
CBHW072153090426
42740CB00012B/2254